T0209763

FEELING GOOD WITH POETRY

Healing Poems for Children

Written By
Mira Williams

Illustration
Grace Jieren Zhang

Copyright © 2019 Mirijana Cvetkovic.

All rights reserved. No part of this book may be used or reproduced by any means, graphic, electronic, or mechanical, including photocopying, recording, taping or by any information storage retrieval system without the written permission of the author except in the case of brief quotations embodied in critical articles and reviews.

Interior Image Credit: Grace Jieren Zhang

Balboa Press books may be ordered through booksellers or by contacting:

Balboa Press
A Division of Hay House
1663 Liberty Drive
Bloomington, IN 47403
www.balboapress.com.au
1 (877) 407-4847

Because of the dynamic nature of the Internet, any web addresses or links contained in this book may have changed since publication and may no longer be valid. The views expressed in this work are solely those of the author and do not necessarily reflect the views of the publisher, and the publisher hereby disclaims any responsibility for them.

Any people depicted in stock imagery provided by Getty Images are models, and such images are being used for illustrative purposes only.
Certain stock imagery © Getty Images.

ISBN: 978-1-5043-1673-6 (sc)
ISBN: 978-1-5043-1674-3 (e)

Print information available on the last page.

Balboa Press rev. date: 03/07/2019

BALBOA.
PRESS
A DIVISION OF HAY HOUSE

FEELING GOOD WITH POETRY

To my family and my friends,
To beginnings and to ends.
To the future and the past,
To great love that's unsurpassed.
To the creator that's within us all,
To those who always seem to fall.
This book is dedicated to you,
Peace and love and all that's true.

THE WALL

Came across a wall today,
Tall and looming in every way.
Tried to climb over the top,
Scratched and scraped it's every spot.

Something tapped me from behind,
Not knowing their name but they were kind.
Offered to help me get over the wall,
Even leant a hand so I wouldn't fall.

Started my climb with them by my side,
Kind enough so I could confide.
All of my fears and all of my doubts,
All of my worries and anger bouts.

Came across a ridge I froze,
Took a chance and then I rose.
Over this ridge that stopped me from,
Continuing my path from here on.

This being I met stood with me,
As I kept walking until I was free.
Of that ridge on the wall of gloom,
Kept walking until I felt no doom.

Reached the top was proud as punch,
Thanked my new friend a whole bunch.
Then they were gone like ice did they melt,
Yet always there if ever I need help.

LONELY DESPAIR SAD SHAME UPSET
WORRING DOUBT ?? GUILT HOSTILE HATE
PAIN STRESS DISHONEST FRUSTRATION FEAR
RACISM
ORANT PREJUDICE ENVY REGRET ANXIOUS JEALO

LOVE YOURSELF

Love yourself for who you are,
Your spots, your skin and your scars.
You're the story in your own play,
Don't let yourself get in your own way.

Appreciate the things you do,
What are your talents, what can you do?
Can you dance can you sing?
Do you write what's your thing?

Follow the dreams you love,
Don't delay this message from above.
The universe is all around us you know?
Always vibrating fast and never slow.

Love yourself friends from afar,
You're a magnificent shining star.
Love will heal everything its true,
Heal them, me and of course you!

DARKNESS WITHIN

Deep within it will raise its head,
When least expected you'll feel its dread.
Inside is where the light won't break,
But listen here to what's not fake.

You have the power you know you do,
Change your thoughts stop feeling blue.
I know you think this lines not true,
But the light is always within you.

Decide today to change your habits,
Of negative thoughts that breed like rabbits.
Stand your ground on all things good,
Breathe deep and be peaceful as you should.

Away! Away! Darkness within,
Because in the end you know I will win.

EYE ON THE PRIZE

Eyes on the prize I'm focused as hell,
I'll get through and then I'll tell,
My story from the start to end,
How I overcame this challenge friend.

Took my mind away from the bad,
Focused on things that didn't make me sad.
Watched funny movies and sang silly songs,
Did happy things all day long.

Rolled with the punches that came my way,
But never ever did I stray.
Kept my eye on that golden prize,
It was big but my perfect size.

Achieved my goal and felt the shift,
Got my prize oh what a gift!
Worth the struggle and the strain,
Saying goodbye to all the pain.

FORGIVENESS

Lovingly forgive those who hurt you,
You know better than they do.
Each on a journey of their own,
They can't understand on a lower tone.

The tone of vibration is what we mean,
The higher you go the happier you'll be.
If you're not there it's hard to stay,
Around those who are there every day.

So align yourself with good feeling thoughts,
You will reap the benefits of course.
Wait a little for all to be clear,
Your happy outcome will appear.

BUTTERFLIES

Butterflies fluttering here and there,
Living life freely without a care,
Back to source within fourteen days,
Trusting the process in every way.

Not a care in the world flying the skies above,
Living life freely surrounded by love,
Enjoying flowers in the garden of life,
Never thinking they'd be in strife.

Magical colours their wings ensue,
Purple, green, yellow, pink and blue.
Making me smile when they fly by,
Opens my heart time after time.

Lessons they give tell us to be,
Happy and loving with all you see.
Live the fullest life whenever you can,
Don't forget where your spirit began.

ENERGY WITHIN

Feeling happy deep inside,
That's the energy within.
When your heart soars and starts to fly,
That's the energy within.

When you're scared and alone,
That's the energy within.
When you don't feel like you're home.
That's the energy within.

The anticipation of something new,
That's the energy within.
Reaching peace you've focused on true,
That's the energy within.

When you feel uncertain in a haze,
That's the energy within.
When you're depressed for many days,
That's the energy within.

Energy within is any feeling you choose,
Are your feelings a win or are they a lose?
It's up to you to guide its way,
Choose wisely spirit and do it today.

TENSION BE GONE

Stomach feels tight,
There's tension in sight.
Starting to make me stress.

Control has been lost,
Been feeling quite cross,
Not able to do my best.

Let feelings pass you by,
Like clouds in the sky.
Focus on the prize.

It's all down to you,
What I say is true,
Be resilient and be wise.

FREEDOM

Choose freedom in your life today,
No matter what don't ever stray.
A new day's here it's time to rejoice,
You can do this it's your choice.

Affirm you're always free to do,
Anything that you want to.
Make it a priority today,
Life is fun go out and play.

Go out now and find your bliss,
Enjoy the things you thought you'd miss.
Go let loose and be free,
Like a fish swimming at sea.

Let the wind blow through your hair,
Do it today without a care.
Every day is precious my friend,
Never let your freedom end.

CREATOR OF MINE

Child of my creator is what I am,
Loving and pure knowing I can,
Believe in something I cannot see,
But feel it? Yes! That's why I believe.

No matter how many tough days there are,
Each of them much better by far.
I'm deserving of that I create,
Think of my dreams and meditate.

Good things will always be around you,
Depending on what you decide to do.
Take a stand and make a promise to self,
Don't let your dreams lay sitting on the shelf.

DEEP DOWN
I'M FREE

Can't escape this feeling of dread,
So tired of being in my head.
Decide to breathe deep and slow,
Relax, don't think but go with the flow.

Feeling the dread start to shift and break,
Into a better place for my own sake.
Little by little I focus on peace,
Until I'm back in my space of ease.

Although a little still remains,
Keep on doing this again and again.
It will come to me that's a universal law,
I'm free in my heart I know this for sure.

Feeling free is my goal,
It's freedom that heals the soul.
Life is full of life once again,
No more dread no more strain.

PEACE WITH LIFE

Calm all around the peace is here,
Whispering quietly in your ear.
You are wonderful you are great,
You're unique like a snowflake.

Survived the storm now time to teach,
There's better places you can reach,
Your dreams and aspirations too,
Anything you want is available to you.

Walk through life with head held high,
Be the example for others to fly.
As you are in this present space,
Guide them into a brighter place.

Step with life's glorious beat,
A rhythm of love that's truly sweet.
Be whoever you want to be,
In doing this you will fly free.

LOVE CHANGES
LIFE

Notice the negativity around?
Saw some today and this is what I found.
People don't realise their impact on others,
Mothers, fathers, sisters and brothers.

Looked at them and saw they don't know,
What I know about universal flow.
If they did they'd change their tune,
I hope people embrace love real soon.

Loving of self is a good start,
Love flows around within your heart.
Helping you see the divine within,
With love around you'll always win.

Changing your life this word love does,
Flying free like a thousand doves.
Into the air as free as can be,
You, your love and universal energy.

When love's change does appear,
People will begin to release their fear.
Treat each other with kindness too,
Stop the negative taking over you.

OVERCOMING FEAR

It's not fair! It's not fair!
Why is it here again in the air?
Thought I'd left the fear behind,
Now it's back for the second time.

Blaming myself for this mess,
Doing nothing but giving me stress.
So tired of the trouble and despair,
Want to give up throw hands in the air.

Giving up is just not me,
Gotta dig in deep to be free.
Sure my strength can sometimes waiver,
Centre myself and pray to my saviour.

Knowing that this too shall end,
It's up to me to defend,
My honour and seeing dreams come true,
I'll overcome and see this through.

MIRACLE

Is this miracle here?
Do I really feel it near?
Pray to the universe every day,
Hard still as my thoughts can stray.

Too much thinking blocking the lines,
Start to feel negative most of the time.
Reminding self it will be okay,
Have faith dear one help's on the way.

Your thoughts create remember this,
Leading you to a life of bliss.
Stand your ground on what you desire,
Let it burn inside like a wild fire.

No rushing as you'll reach the end,
Follow the light my dear friend.
Your miracle is truly on its way,
Appearing soon now perhaps today.

ANGER TO PEACE

I'm so angry don't know what to do,
Needing a miracle but hoping for two.
Beating my head and asking why,
Why do I feel this all of the time?

Don't know how to calm the beast,
It breathes fire and has unleashed.
Feel so angry at everything,
Lost joy in my voice to even sing.

Beat my pillow and let it go,
Felt much better now I know,
How to move it out of me,
Expel the energy more safely.

Looked inside and saw the raw me,
Saw the person I'm meant to be.
Moving away from anger to peace,
Knowing the anger will finally cease.

REACH FOR YOUR GREAT

Sometimes I don't know how to get,
To a calm place I can reset.
But chipping away every day,
Gets me to that place of play.

On top of the thoughts that are dark,
Replacing them with a brighter spark.
Feeling the cloud start to lift,
Loving the feeling of a positive shift.

Look at the world with clearer eyes,
The beauty around does inspire.
The magic that is within me,
It's in you too and that you'll see.

Hang in there and reach for your great,
Step by step you must take.
Little by little every day,
Is the key that lights the way.

YOU CAN DO IT

Why so many questions?
I ask myself.
Is this a lesson?
Do I need help?

Some days I just want to hide away,
From the world just for one day.
Digging in deep I get dressed,
Put on my shoes and Sunday best.

Walk out the door greeted by the sun,
Birds are singing, having fun.
"That will be me!" I think to myself,
Now focus on that will bring me wealth.

Not the money but peace for you,
Anyone can do it, it's easy to do.
Remember the mother who led the way,
Her legacy continues to this day.

WHEN YOU'RE BLUE

I lost my motivation,
Don't know what to do.
Hating the place I'm in,
Making me feel dark blue.

It's okay to feel blue,
A colour part of you,
But don't forget the rest,
Combined you'll feel the best.

Mix it with sparkly yellow,
Or brightly coloured pink.
A splash of green and purple,
Would be nice don't you think?

Time will come when it is easy,
Colours within will feel light and breezy.
No rushing ahead will wait and see,
That which you create will certainly be.

Monitor your feelings,
They'll help its true.
To get you to that place,
That no longer feels so blue.

MOVING TO BETTER

A leap of faith into something new,
Is what you have to try and do.
A bigger picture is in sight,
Believe it's there with all your might.

Take a leap of faith to it,
Never doubt fully commit.
Good things will come to you dear one,
Don't forget it's meant to be fun!

It might look a little grim right now,
That's all in your head and I'll show you how.
To be successful starts with you,
Positive thoughts through and through.

Believe you are worthy of the best,
This the ingredient to true success.
Roll with the punches and the falls,
Don't beat your head on brick walls.

It will get easier each step you take,
To this new thing you wish to create.
Universal power is there for you,
To support and make your new come true.

FRIENDS

Friends come and friends go,
In and out of the flow.
Some will always want to stay,
Other will just fly away.

When friends attack they are in pain,
Deep inside they hide their shame.
And sadness of a moment lost,
Not realising what it has cost.

If they go then set them free,
Live a full life with joy and glee.
Doesn't matter how they see you,
You know inside it isn't true.

Feels bad knowing it has ended,
Now they've gone you're no longer befriended.
Send them love and on their way,
Better friends will show up some day.

So here's the lesson for you all,
Friendships bust-big and small.
If you want to be a good friend,
Be one yourself until the end.

Printed in the United States
By Bookmasters